SPRING MORNING SUN

Haiku

by

Tom Tico

Spring Morning Sun, Haiku, Tom Tico

Acknowledgments to *American Haiku, Haiku West, Modern Haiku, Dragonfly, Cicada, Inkstone, High/Coo, frogpond, Woodnotes, Brussels Sprout,* and *The Persimmon Tree.*

Cover painting by Mary Fields

Cover design by Jeff Brain

Typesetting by Typesetting Etc., San Francisco

ISBN: 1-57502-711-9

Library of Congress Card Catalog Number: 97-91423

Published by
BELLTOWER PRESS
721 18th Ave.
San Francisco, CA 94121

Printed in the USA by

MORRIS PUBLISHING
3212 East Highway 30 • Kearney, NE 68847 • 1-800-650-7888

Introduction

Although I started writing haiku in 1965 and I've written steadily from then on, I haven't until now published a volume of my poems. The setting for most of them is San Francisco, a city I've lived in practically my whole life, a beautiful place that lends itself to the writing of haiku.

From 1985 through 1996 I spent over seven years in a state of homelessness, sleeping in a redwood forest in Golden Gate Park. Although this period was a challenge, it didn't prevent me from enjoying the leisure of my days. Quite a few of the haiku in this collection spring from that situation.

To have haiku experiences and to be able to turn them into haiku poems, is, and has always been for me an immense satisfaction. And I'm grateful to all those who have inspired me, in particular, Harold Henderson, R. H. Blyth, Walt Whitman, Swami Vivekananda, the Holy Mother, and Ramakrishna.

—Tom Tico

The pavement handprint
invites the neighborhood boys
to try it for size

Aglow with spring sun,
the small girl quietly sways
in the hula hoop . . .

Butterflies flit near . . .
dragons dance in the distance . . .
the old kiting hill

A wisp of spring cloud
drifting apart from the rest . . .
slowly evaporates

A slender maiden
strolls amid falling blossoms
in the tea garden . . .

The old carving tree . . .
a new pair of initials
and the first young leaves

High in the cypress
a multicolored kite—
the evening sky

Mud-puddle water
going this way and that—
spring wind

Stepping lightly by,
past our front-yard irises,
her shapely long legs

After long trudging
on the sun-baked trail—
shade, ferns, and stream

All along the trail
that winds down to the sea—
wild irises!

After gazing at stars . . .
now, I adjust to the rocks
under my sleeping bag

First days of summer . . .
already the leaves gather
beneath the sycamores

The faded fence—
its pickets tied together
with glistening webs

On a flight of stairs
a small boy and an old man
share the evening sun

Chinatown

Age-old odors
  assault the nostrils in Chinatown,
    frail wind-chimes tinkling . . .

Chinatown market:
  picking snow peas one by one—
    old yellow fingers

The old Chinaman
  plies the customers . . .
    hand-carved sages look on

Under dragon-lanterns
the hum of cars, and sing-song
of an ancient tongue

At the alley's end,
amid bustling Chinatown . . .
a cache of bamboo

A working day through . . .
  above Park Presidio
    a hawk circling high . . .

On the pond, ripples . . .
  and the clip-clop of horses
    from beyond the reeds

Coming round the bend,
  and looking for the old pine
    that's no longer there

Unheard since childhood,
yet still singing of the sea . . .
the dusty cowrie shell

Moistening dry lips
while viewing the endless waves:
the taste of the sea

Knee-deep in the sea,
my small son dances and laughs
as the waves gather . . .

Dawn sky, faintly pink . . .
  the mad cackle of blackbirds
    in the lake's tall reeds

In the color and taste
  of the pomegranate seeds:
    the Old Testament

From the two pennies
  my sons threw in the wishing pool
    rings that intersect . . .

A forecast of rain:
as I deliver the mail
. . . the darkening sky

With the children gone
the fall wind opens and closes
the playhouse door

A separation . . .
this fall night I feel
the bed's cold side

a lonely park path . . .
only my grinding footsteps
and the birds' silence

Autumn evening . . .
the last sunlight scaling
the brick wall

The old brass lantern
is doing a wild wind dance
with the autumn moon . . .

Now rising above
the steady pour of the rain:
the rush of the wind

The old neighborhood:
the gang all gone, but the names
still in the cement

Another issue . . .
and the old poet's poems
are missing again

The old hell-raiser
now knows the whole neighborhood
from his window view

autumn evening . . .
the convent's higher windows
being latched-shut

On every step
of the old stone stairway—
autumn leaves

Beside the tenement
a box of broken glass
filled with autumn sun

Two homely people
arm in arm on Market Street
laughing together

Misty autumn rain . . .
In a tenderloin hotel
old men watch TV

Wind-Chimes

Working with the wind,
  the spider hooks his lines
    to the rusty chimes

The glistening web
  vibrates with every tinkle
    of the brass wind-chimes

The tinkle of chimes
  mingles with the steady fall
    of the autumn rain . . .

After wind and rain
of season upon season . . .
the wind-chimes, fainter

The chain dangles free . . .
below, in the withered grass
the rusty chimes

The lopsided chimes
mended and rehung again,
start to work the wind . . .

Men in business suits
checking the sundial's time
with their wrist watches

The empty playground . . .
an old man scanning the sand
with a metal detector

With the chimes gone . . .
now I heed the silence
of the autumn wind

Wearing a walkman
as he steadily rings his bell—
street-corner Santa

Now, the street empty . . .
beneath drifts of confetti
the days of last year

Early January . . .
gathering on street corners
aging Christmas trees

My aging mother
tells of her happiest moment:
swinging as a child

In my children's room
shafts of winter moonlight
on the empty beds

Bound to his big chair . . .
he watches the twilight come
over the gables

Already it's night . . .
still sinking into the trees
the last of twilight

Over the fireplace,
on the living-room wall—
the fern's shadow

Winter night—
the old dancer
bedridden

How the chimney-sparks
disappear in the darkness
of this stormy night

These cobblestone steps
rise under the three pines
to a city view

A brisk winter day;
drifting from the bakery
the fresh scent of bread

An old street, run-down,
   but one house with two plum trees
      tall and full of bloom

Shining on the belly
   of the laughing Buddha:
      spring morning sun

spring wind!
   tying up the tongue
      of the rusty chimes

The old windmill:
  tilting at its tattered sails
    the winds of spring

Two aged winos
  are sharing a small bottle
    in the spring sunshine . . .

Deep in the alley:
  a single blue iris
    blooms in the shadows

In the mission garden
amid the shadows and ivy—
old Spanish markers

The old wine cellar:
still the flickering shadows
and the touch of webs

Drumming steadily . . .
the old beekeeper waits
for the searching swarm

Picking golden plums
in the sunny high branches . . .
the taste of summer

As the ripples fade
from my wishing-pool penny,
the returning moon

Above the gables
and the criss-cross of wires—
the pale summer moon

In the presidio,
concrete fortifications
yield to incoming fog

Under every tree
on this street of swirling fog
a circle of drops

Through the two arches
of the old stone bridge—nothing,
but the rising mist

Tassajara Zen Center

Deep in the mountains,
  at the monastery gate
    a view of stars!

Beyond the boulders
  where the stream becomes a pool
    morning butterflies

Autumn evening . . .
lighting the kerosene lamp
as the cabin dims

All of a sudden,
in the night's utter stillness
chimes begin to play . . .

The steep winding road—
returning to the world
through a burnt forest

Dropping out . . .
  my key ring
    dwindling

Above the gable
  of the old Victorian:
    the gathering dusk

All by herself now,
  the old woman rocking
    the autumn wind

first autumn rain . . .
inside, listening to the music
of a bygone era . . .

Autumn moonlight . . .
climbing the white cottage door
a moth and its shadow

In the dead of night—
the sound of running feet
from the street below

Vanishing within
the waters of the old pool—
autumn twilight

In the backyard of Gus's Pub:
drunk with stars!

Leaving her house
after a one-night stand . . .
the autumn mist

Heavy autumn rain . . .
into the night men labor
on a collapsed street

Drizzly afternoon . . .
dropping the mouse and mousetrap
into the garbage can

Scattered about
on the storm-darkened streets—
broken umbrellas

a gray winter day;
music from the carousel
drifts through the playground

In the tea garden,
the high arch of the old bridge
spans an empty pool

As the evening wanes,
the houses on the hillside
as their lights go on . . .

The last plum petals
sift thru the budding branches
of the bent cherry . . .

Every now and then
I glance from the haiku page:
poolside irises

Shining in the pool
at the feet of St. Francis:
spring morning sun

Spring
pacing
inside

An early spring rain;
inside, reading the haiku
of an old master

Spring rain:
even the oil-slicks
have bloomed

Saturday morning . . .
in the gable's high niches
the pigeons cooing . . .

In the living room,
the stained-glass window aglow
with spring morning sun

Shining on my mother
as she sits in her great chair:
the spring morning sun

As with my father . . .
now, in my mother's sickroom
the smell of old age

a cloudy spring day;
the branch appears and disappears
on the sickroom shade

The neglected yard . . .
now the lilies are blooming
amid blackberry vines

On Mother's Day
cutting all of the lilies
for her last bouquet

All through the night,
after my mother's passing—
the sound of foghorns

In the mission garden,
the old fountain overflows
with morning-glories

So swiftly it fades
  the luminous blue color
    of the dawning sky

The hawk that settled
  on top of the tall cypress
    now drifts with the wind

For a moment,
  lost in the sun
    the freewheeling hawk

Lingering
in the folds of the lace curtains
the glow of sunrise

The rusty wind-chimes
   wait quietly for the music
      of a summer breeze . . .

With the passing years . . .
   even the scar she gave me
      has faded away

After a few drinks
  of the heated sake—
    the floating world

As day breaks . . .
  the lightness of her breath
    on my back

Lunchtime . . .
  from the unfinished house
    wolf whistles

A moon-viewing party:
   only the hot sake
      and the cold fog

fog
and foghorns
silence the city

a morning of fog:
   not a bird sings, but a dog
      barking and yelping

Deepening the mist:
the steamy window
of the old cafe

Despite garbled words
her eyes still greet me
with their usual warmth

Dusk . . .
at the end of this long street—
vanishing cypresses

In the interval
between night and day—
the cawing of crows

a morning of fog:
walking alone on a street
with no end in sight

In a vacant lot,
a broken television
faces an empty couch

On a wintry street
every person's breath becomes
a part of the mist

Beneath a picture
of old Chinatown: Chinese girls
eat burgers and fries

In the Li Po bar,
watching the clientele drink,
a golden buddha

Last night's words . . .
this morning's silence . . .

Expressionless
as she puts on
her face

Nothing to bring her . . .
except flowers from gardens
all along the way

Through the peephole
a prism of morning sun
speckles the white wall

peephole:
an eyeful
of sun

Lighting up every glass
in the crystal cabinet—
spring morning sun

Dappling my hands:
age-spots
and a light spring rain

The young girl's fingers
  explore the lacy fibers
    of a skeleton leaf

The water that pours
  from the hands of St. Francis
    slakes the hummingbirds

The weight of the pack
lightened by the wildflowers
that border the trail

Just riding the wind,
the red-tailed hawk soars
higher and higher

After the embers die,
I turn my attention
to the starry sky

(at the beach)
Becoming a part
of every haiku I read:
the sound of the sea

Sandpipers
running along the glassy beach
on top of themselves

The fallen petals
mingle with the smooth stones
we picked at the beach

In this summer heat,
only the morning-glories
retain their coolness

Exacerbating
this midday heat—
the crow's caw . . .

Heat wave—
a war being waged
with water balloons

Watching my son
as he plays basketball . . .
seeing my own moves

Waiting for the ferry . . .
from the pier I watch the crabs
crawling among the rocks

As the sun moves up
the winding steps
so do I

After the earthquake
the shaking continues
in my girlfriend's voice

Aftershock—
the candleflame
flickers

autumn
in the old whistler's
vibrato

a morning of fog:
  again and again the caw
    of an unseen crow

Into old pots and pans
  thrown out in the backyard—
    the musical rain

Haiku gathering . . .
  after a bowl of lentils
    Basho and Buson

The long stone stairway
has led to this secluded world
of blossoming plum trees

Beneath darkening skies
the flowers of the plum tree
whiter and whiter

a windless morning
and still the plum blossoms
flutter to the ground

Early April—
the little girl in the swing
learning to pump . . .

springtime . . .
idling in front of the projects:
old black men

a gorgeous sunset;
the seller of incense
gives me a free stick

Finally sloughing off
the black and silvery clouds—
the pale yellow moon

As I read haiku,
the bedroom's shaded window
brightening with dawn

Beneath the lily-pads
the shimmering cherry trees
that surround the pond

The old fountain
with its water jetting up
into the spring rain

Engulfing
the purple rhododendrons
shadows of evening

Dusk . . .
the whole forest dark
except for the lilies

homeless:
no keys

In Golden Gate Park
all alone on a trail
of dappled moonlight

Passing clouds . . .
in a grove of redwoods
wavering moonlight

Under the redwoods
I join the moonlight
in my sleeping bag

Quietly waiting
for the bakery to open,
the early risers

coffee shop:
the newspaper
communion

power outage . . .
in the coffee shop's bathroom
the soft candlelight

At the soup kitchen,
a faded reproduction
of *the Last Supper*

after a long day
the teeter-totter
at rest in twilight

Even the fallen petals
of the magnolia tree
aglow with moonlight

the short night—
in my dream surfing
wave after wave

Gray skies at dawn . . .
the morning-glories linger
in their violet phase

Sunbathing . . .
not seeing but feeling
each passing cloud

On the redwood stump,
across its numerous rings—
the snail's silvery trail

a sweltering day;
on the open window's sill
the bulldog's heavy head

At the nude beach:
even without the costumes
the same old roles

Beyond the chitchat
of the garden party—
the mockingbird's song

Climbing over
her front-yard fence:
passion flowers

Sounds of cool jazz . . .
as twilight deepens
through shades of blue

One foot jutting out
from his cardboard covering;
the first morning light

Now a street person
but still in combat fatigues—
the Vietnam vet

Over the park dwellers,
flying from a shopping cart—
the stars and stripes

In an autumn wind,
  looking through a box of books
    left on the corner

As the month ends . . .
  the line at the soup kitchen
    longer every day . . .

For just a moment,
  across my field of vision—
    my gray, windblown hair

From the picture shop—
Rembrandt gazing pensively
at the punk rockers

Shortening the line
at the soup kitchen—
the first fall rain

The China exhibit:
more vibrant than bamboo
this painting of it

a lonely park path . . .
the tall plumes of pampas grass
deepen the twilight

Drifting away
in the moonlit redwoods,
my misty breath . . .

In my sleeping bag
in a fetal position;
this cold autumn night

As the sky lightens,
  the tall plumes of pampas grass
    flower in the mist

Etched in the sidewalk,
  the peace symbol encompasses
    a few fallen leaves

Walking late at night . . .
  again and again my shadow
    lengthens and vanishes

In predawn silence,
as I walk beside the park—
a cough from the bushes

Hovering over
a city of flickering lights—
the full autumn moon

This long autumn night—
noticing the first wrinkles
in my son's forehead

The caw of a crow
from one of these cypresses
that jut from the rocks

A crash of thunder!
Swiftly the sky darkens
with shrieking crows

One after another
crows vanish into the dark
branches of the cypress

Winter sunshine:
beneath the bare branches
a maze of shadows

The old widower:
so reluctant to conclude
the conversation

Shopping
for his own casket—
the cancer patient

Out of the darkness
the quiet intensity
of the beggar's plea

Housesitting . . .
acquainting myself with the books
and the cats

After homelessness . . .
how different the rain looks
from a cosy room

Completing
   the rock garden
      these fallen leaves

More and more
   the fallen leaves . . .
      age-spots on my hands

Looking for the bird
   that sang a moment ago
      in the bare branches . . .

Into the back
of the pickup truck
plum petals fall . . .

Falling
  as gently as the rain,
    plum petals

After the last storm,
  even in the rain puddle—
    blue sky & white clouds

Wet dream;
the first day
of spring

The start of spring—
telling her it's too painful
to see her as a friend

Playing havoc
with my cowl—
spring wind

Through the holes
of her fashionably torn pants—
drops of spring rain

Spring rain:
bringing out the sheen
on the snail's shell

An old bottlecap:
now just a little pool
of freshly fallen rain

Memorial Day:
the Vietnam vet
ironing the flag

Tied
to the veteran's crutch—
a miniature flag

Passing through the crowd
  as the Blue Angels perform—
    monarch butterfly

On a quiet street,
giving voice to the morning mist:
the pigeons cooing . . .

At the school yard,
volleyballs rising and falling
through the morning mist

Looking both ways
as I cross the street,
the deepening mist

Summer breeze:
  this dappled path
    in constant flux

On the grass, passed out . . .
  Slowly his covering changes
    from sun to shadow

So many days now
  the absence of the old man
    who sat in the sun

Briefly at rest
before the next round—
carousel horses

After the frog leaps,
the ripples are still spreading
in the old pond . . .

Beside her backpack
and her rolled-up sleeping bag:
the *Tao Te Ching*

Though far from the beach
the tangy scent of the sea
in this swirling fog

From the sand dollar
I used as a paperweight—
a trickle of beach

Winding along
the coast highway—
the edge of the sea

Late summer morning:
from the recovery house
the sound of chanting

During Sunday mass:
a recovering alcoholic
drinks the blood of Christ

The inner city . . .
On Sycamore Street
not a single tree

The inner city . . .
attached to the chain-link fence
a collage of hubcaps

Out of oily asphalt
abstract expressionism
in an autumn rain

Playing in the rubble
where the projects were—
black kids

Autumn evening;
before we separate
one last meeting

The next morning:
rereading the last page
of the happy ending

Dark night:
gazing more intensely
at Van Gogh's *Sunflowers*

This autumn night
  the suicide bridge
    shrouded in fog

Walking late at night . . .
  the wariness between me
    and the passing stranger

Beyond the rim
  of my black umbrella—
    this gray day

On an empty street,
   the last music of the night
      from the unseen chimes

Nativity scene:
   the statues set
      in real hay

Christmas Eve . . .
   at the lot, the trees
      not chosen

Deeper this year
the ruts in the path
to my sleeping place

My mummy bag
as it warms up
the stars

Just a patch of sky,
yet large enough to frame
the meteor's flight

Garage sale . . .
  Taking one last look
    at my Renoir prints

Waiting in line
  at the soup kitchen,
    reading Issa

Critiquing the cuisine
  at the soup kitchen—
    two homeless men

On a friend's sofa,
envisioning my place in the park—
this cold rainy night

a morning of mist
the subdued sound of the birds
on this quiet street

His white tapping cane . . .
and the rustle of windblown leaves
along the sidewalk

foghorns . . .
only the nothingness
where the steeples stand

Through the great window
a panoramic view
of the fog

Out of the fog
first the ridge of pines
and then the mountains

This long endless night . . .
above the gables the sky
lightens to lavender

full in the face
of the old Victorian:
spring morning sun

As I leave the clinic
after testing negative—
the sun and sky

The pizza seller:
 on the back of her T-shirt
 You are not the body

Through the lace curtains
 dappling her face and gown
 the moon's pale light

After the stars fade
 and the street-lights go out,
 this quiet morning

almost unnoticed
beneath the rhododendrons
the forget-me-nots

Lingering
in a valley of flowers
morning mist

Surrounded by flowers,
yet I gaze at the trail
that winds to the woods

At the monastery,
all of their recycling
in perfect order

Seeing its shadow—
I seek its fluttering form
in the sunlit sky

Each time I glance
from the haiku page—
a new cloud formation

In playground sand
before the children arrive
the tracks of birds

After I inhale
the fragrance of the white rose,
a girl smiles at me

At the burial,
with every waft of the wind—
the scent of jasmine

Memorial Day:
wave after wave
hitting the beach

Changing my course:
flowering eucalyptus
in a clear blue sky

The white butterfly
just the touch of my shadow
and it flies away

Barely visible
beneath the morning-glories—
the chain-link fence

Pulling me away
from a world of pure fiction—
the squawk of a jay

Divorced years ago . . .
but the pine that we planted
towers over her yard

The old workshop:
the color of autumn
in his rusted saw

and still it stands
with neither its bells
nor its stained glass

Becoming a part
of the night's utter stillness,
the soft fall of rain

In my viewless room:
hanging a landscape
of deep autumn woods

Into the basement
to resurrect my books—
the touch of webs

New reading glasses
with greater magnification—
autumn deepens

Overhead the stars
but far to the west—
remnants of sunset

Construction site:
  the gigantic crane
    juts into the stars

Swaying in the wind,
  the tall plumes of pampas grass
    sweep the starry sky

Misting across
the cold bright stars—
my own breath

Enlivening
the last vestiges of night—
the morning birds

Bursting around me
as I near the wildflowers—
monarch butterflies!

At the occult shop:
the wizard's crystal ball
catches the morning sun

Illuminating
the bell and the belltower—
spring morning sun

Up where the path peaks
the cherry trees flowering
amid the white clouds

Above the city
in a wilderness of sky—
the freewheeling hawk

Inside, swimming laps . . .
Spring's flowery scent
through an open door

Fluttering briefly
over the sundial's face—
monarch butterfly

The wind-chimes silent
    but the tongue sways gently
        in the evening breeze

Amid the dark leaves
    the white hydrangeas
        mirroring the moon

Adding a faint glow
    to the early morning light
        old-fashioned street lamps

Afterword

I dreamt I was browsing through my books and came upon Blyth's four volumes of *Haiku* and two volumes of *A History of Haiku*. But instead of the beige covers that Blyth's books have, these had exquisitely done black covers, each one marked with a unique and colorful design. As I looked through the books I realized that they were incredibly old and must be handled with considerable care. It was as if they were ancient scrolls, full of the highest art and wisdom.

I dreamt that many gifts from Japan had come to me through the years, but I hadn't opened them. Finally I decided to, and once I had started I didn't know why I hadn't opened the gifts earlier. There were also a number of gifts from Harold Henderson. They too were clearly a part of the gifts from Japan. There was a big bottle of sake that I wished I had opened when I was still drinking—because now I was no longer interested in it. I was pleased and grateful for the gifts that had been given me, and I realized that I should convey my thanks to all the givers.